VISIONS OF BARRY

Jeffery Grayer

www.crecy.co.uk

First published in 2016 by Crécy Publishing

A CIP record for this book is available from the British Library

Printed in Slovenia by GPS Print

ISBN 9781909328495

Crécy Publishing Limited
1a Ringway Trading Estate, Shadowmoss Road, Manchester M22 5LH
www.crecy.co.uk

Cover captions
Front
Main image **It is hard to believe that the splendour that is currently the operational** *Tangmere* **was once in such a state.**
Small image **'Vivid Rust' is now the livery worn by this Standard Class 2MT 2-6-0.**

Back
Main image **In company with 'Jinty' No. 47279 Standard Class 2 2-6-0 No. 78018 was still substantially complete, apart from smashed cab window glass and a liberal coating of rust, in this view taken shortly after the locomotive's arrival in June 1967 having been withdrawn from Shrewsbury shed the previous November. Achieving fame as the locomotive stuck in the snow in the famous BTF film** *Snowdrift at Bleath Gill* **this was one of four of the class to be stabled at Barry, this example leaving the yard in November 1978 for the Market Bosworth preservation centre at Shackerstone. It was subsequently sold on to the Darlington Railway Preservation Society and it is currently awaiting final reassembly at Loughborough.**
Small image **Battle of Britain No 34070** *Manston*.

Right **Sold for £9,000 plus VAT in September 1978, and liberally decorated with 'Keep Off' and 'Reserved' warnings, Maunsell S15 No 30847, the final 4-6-0 locomotive of the type to be built by the Southern Railway, receives attention from a couple of paintbrush-wielding preservationists from the Maunsell Locomotive Society. This shot was taken shortly before the locomotive's removal in October 1978, after some fourteen years in the yard, to the Bluebell Railway, where a return to steam took place in October 1992. After a further overhaul the locomotive re-entered traffic in December 2013.**

CONTENTS

Introduction	4	S15	44	Eastern Region	92
The Yard	6	Bulleid Light Pacific	48	B1	92
Cheek by Jowl	12	Merchant Navy	59	BR Standard classes	93
Western Region	28	In close-up	64	Duke of Gloucester	93
Castle	28	Monochrome interlude	72	Class 4 4-6-0	94
Pannier tank	32	Midland Region	78	Class 2 2-6-0	95
2884 Class 2-8-0	33	4F	78	Class 4 2-6-4T	96
Manor	34	'Jinty'	80	Class 9F 2-10-0	99
Hall	36	Ivatt tank	82	Diesels	102
7200 Class 2-8-2T	37	Stanier 8F	83	Freight stock	104
4200 Class 2-8-0T	38	Jubilee	85	Down the road at Newport	110
Prairie tank	39	Ivatt Class 2	86	Preservation postscript	113
Southern Region	40	'Crab'	88	Barry factfile	116
Mogul	40	S&D 7F	90	Index	118

INTRODUCTION

Dai Woodham's Barry scrapyard continues to exert a fascination 25 years after the final locomotive, Churchward 4575 Class Prairie tank No 5553, left the yard in January 1990. I, like many another enthusiast, visited the yard on several occasions from the mid-1960s through to the 1980s. The images herein were taken during these visits, initially in black and white and latterly in colour. The lines of rusting locomotives became increasingly more decrepit as time passed thanks to the effects of the sea air, the attention of vandals and those more concerned with salvaging removable parts for eventual restoration of their own favourite types. That combination of decaying metal

ESTABLISHED 1892   TELEPHONE: BARRY **3136/7**

WOODHAM BROS.
(INCORPORATING THE BARRY DOCK MARINE STORE COMPANY)

PARTNERS :
D. WOODHAM
A. WOODHAM
P. WOODHAM
W. WOODHAM

GENERAL MERCHANTS

Bankers :
National Provincial Bank Ltd.   **54a THOMPSON STREET,**
BARRY, GLAM.

carcasses juxtaposed with sprouting vegetation against a background of light and shadow often combined to produce interesting photographic possibilities. More than 200 locomotives were rescued from oblivion, many having since been restored to working order. With some fifty classes from all BR Regions at one time represented in the yard, since it received its first consignment of ex-GWR locomotives in 1959, this volume does not attempt a comprehensive record, but instead aims to recapture something of the unique atmosphere of the changing scene over the years. My special thanks to contributor George Woods GW, who has filled some gaps in my own photographic record.

Jeffery Grayer
Devon, 2016

Map by kind permission of Ordnance Survey.

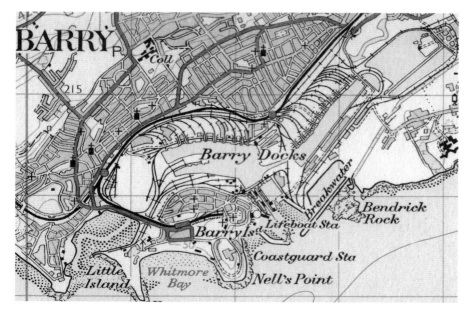

This general panorama of the yard taken in the spring of 1966 shows the scale of the main storage area. I had travelled up from my home in Sussex for the day for my first visit to Barry, but the stories told on the enthusiasts' grapevine could never quite prepare one for the sight of such a collection. Great Western types, many still sporting safety valve bonnets, predominate in this view, but Bulleid Pacific No 34039 *Boscastle*, which had arrived in the yard the previous September, can be discerned on the right.

THE YARD

Against a background of rows of houses on the hill behind the docks at Barry, line after line of rusting hulks greeted the many thousands of visitors to Woodham's yard over the years.

Ships' masts and funnels bear witness to the busy nature of the working docks at Barry, which over the years exported many millions of tons of Welsh coal. From its height in 1913, when more than half of the 57 million tons of coal produced was exported through the South Wales ports, this traffic gradually declined until most of the pits had closed by the 1980s, the last coal having been shipped from Barry in 1976. However, the relaxation of the rules regarding the export of scrap metal made direct loading from Woodham's yard, ideally situated next to extensive docks, into waiting ships a practicable proposition.

The slowly diminishing band of remaining locomotives is glimpsed through the struts of a pedestrian bridge that crossed the yard to the east of the holding sidings.

This yard view dates from 1973 and shows a 45xx Prairie tank and ex-LMS Class 2 at the buffer stops. As is apparent from this view not all the sidings had the luxury of buffer stops so careful shunting techniques had to be employed to avoid running out of track!

The crudely daubed designation on the tender of Standard Class 5 No 73156, photographed on 8 September 1968, leaves no doubt as to its ultimate destination. A label would also be tied to a convenient handrail on the locomotive to ensure delivery to the correct scrapyard. *GW*

This final view of the yard, taken in September 1968, shows among others 'Black 5' No 45491 and Bulleid Pacific No 34027 *Taw Valley*. *GW*

CHEEK BY JOWL

Left **Battle of Britain No 34070** *Manston*.

Below **The brutal removal of a West Country badge from the 'air-smoothed' casing with the clear outline of the nameplate scroll evident above was to be seen on No 34007** *Wadebridge*.

A grass-grown pannier.

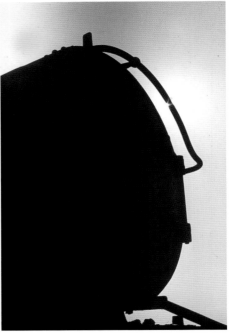

Above **A 'contre-jour' shot with the sun squinting from behind a smokebox handrail.**

Left **The serried ranks of former steam giants contain, among others, Standard tank No 80150 and Stanier 8F No 42859.**

Right and Below **Smokeboxes in close-up – No 78059 and an unidentified Bulleid Pacific.**

Left **A royal rear end – the tender of a King.**

Below **Rusting pannier No 4612.**

Merchant Navy No 35022 *Holland-America Line*, with its cab fittings long gone, has its firehole doors in the open position; in original form these were opened by a treadle powered by steam pressure. Alongside is Standard tank No 80072.

Left **No 34046** *Braunton* **also reveals its firehole doors, this time with North British Type 21 D6122 for company.**

Right and Below **A very dilapidated No 35018** *British India Line* **quietly rusts away in the summer sun.**

Left **Rosebay willowherb adds a spot of colour to the drab scene of Collett 56xx Class No 5637, seen in September 1968.** *GW*

Right **Through a smashed spectacle glass, the overbridge to the south of the site can be seen.** *GW*

With a freshly painted buffer beam and drawhook, but missing a buffer, a Bulleid Pacific waits for rescue.

The houses on the hill behind had a grandstand view of the yard, but their occupants were doubtless relieved to see the site eventually cleared.

Right **The weathered green paintwork of Jubilee No 45699 *Galatea* and an unidentified Manor is countered by the orange tints of rusting metal.**

Below **Now shorn of its chimney and many other parts, this former GWR Manor will no longer be needed for the 'Cambrian Coast Express'.**

An Ivatt tank displays white-painted valve gear and a rather 'Heath Robinson', but nonetheless effective, chimney cover, no doubt in an effort to protect the internal fabric of the locomotive.

One of the four Standard Class 2s that ended up in the yard. Buffers were some of the first items to disappear, legitimately or otherwise, being relatively easily to remove, albeit heavy.

Right and Below **Driver's-eye views.**

WESTERN REGION

Castle

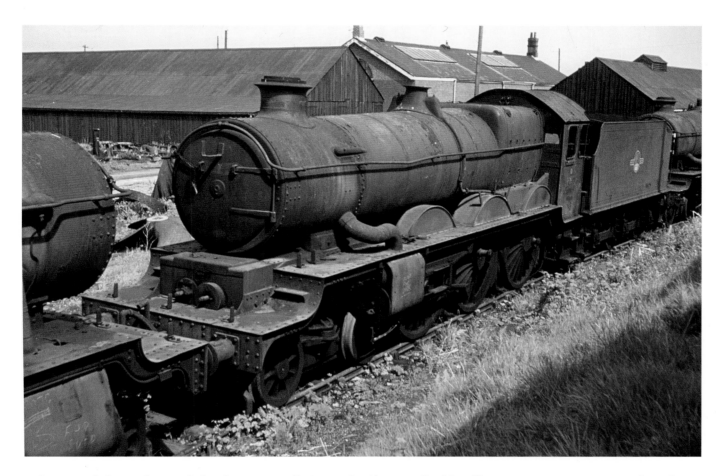

Left **One of the quintet of the famous Collett Castle Class to find itself at Barry was No 7027 *Thornbury Castle*. This view was taken on 14 May 1966, a couple of years after the arrival of the 4-6-0 following withdrawal from service at the end of 1963. Forty-three years on from its exit from the yard in 1972 it remains one of a handful of the first 100 locomotives to be rescued not to have subsequently steamed in preservation. Currently owned by Pete Waterman, it is in store at the Crewe Heritage Centre. *GW***

Above **Also photographed on that day in 1966 was No 5029 *Nunney Castle*, which has since gone on to great things in preservation. *GW***

No 5080, originally named *Ogmore Castle*, was renamed *Defiant* in 1941 after the Boulton Paul Defiant, one of the aircraft instrumental in the Battle of Britain. It spent almost eleven years at Barry before being moved by rail to the Birmingham Railway Museum Trust at Tyseley in August 1974 together with Nos 5637 and 4160. Although initially purchased as a source of spare parts for *Clun Castle*, it was decided to restore the locomotive, a process completed in 1988. It then saw use on a variety of special trains, but since 2002 has been on static display at Quainton Road's reconstructed Oxford Rewley Road station together with GWR special saloon W9001 used by Eisenhower and Churchill during the Second World War.

This further view from May 1966 is of No 5043 *Earl of Mount Edgcumbe*, named after a GWR director, another Castle Class to have changed names, having originally been called *Barbury Castle*. In 2008 it returned to steam, being restored to late 1950s condition with a Hawksworth tender and BR double chimney, hauling trains principally to Stratford and Didcot from its base at Tyseley. *GW*

Pannier tank

This pair of pannier tanks comprises Collett 5700 Class No 4612 with the white paint adornments, and behind it No 3738. No 4612 ended its working life with BR based in South Wales, so did not have too far to travel to Barry. Some 863 examples of this class were built, making them the most prolific locomotive type on the former GWR. Sixteen members of the class have been preserved, with ten coming from London Transport, which used a number after the WR had ceased to find any use for them. Five were saved from Barry, and one, No 9642, from Hayes scrapyard in Bridgend, where it had been used to shunt other withdrawn locomotives.

2884 Class 2-8-0

This 'exploded' view of Collett 2884 Class 2-8-0 No 3845 is prior to the removal of its asbestos boiler lagging, which occurred on the site in 1978. This was a necessary safety precaution, the asbestos having become exposed through corrosion of the boiler cladding. 9F No 92214 is adjacent, the working lives of the two locomotives being a respectable twenty-two years and a derisory six years respectively.

Manor

With 'In Loving Memory' painted on the smokebox door, another Manor, No 7802 *Bradley Manor*, is in a rather worse state than its classmates, once again photographed before asbestos removal rendered them more presentable. It was rescued from Barry in 1979 by the 'Erlestoke Manor Fund' based at the Severn Valley Railway, originally as a source of spare parts for No 7812. However, the owners had a change of heart and in 1983 the decision was taken to return No 7802 to steam, which it duly did in 1993.

Manor Class No 7828 *Odney Manor* was one of eight of the class bought from BR by Woodham's. On 17 June 2011 it was renamed *Norton Manor* after the base of 40 Commando situated alongside the West Somerset Railway, its current owners, at Norton Fitzwarren. The GWR had always intended to give the name *Norton Manor* to a new locomotive, No 7830, but the order for this was cancelled.

Hall

Above **Modified Hall No 7927 *Willington Hall* looks quite presentable in the sidings at Barry prior to removal for initial preservation at the Swindon & Cricklade Railway.**

Left **The final allocation for Collett 4900 Class Hall No 5952 *Cogan Hall* was Cardiff East Dock. Stored at the Oswestry site of the Cambrian Railways Trust, it was the Trust's intention to restore it. However, in 2010 it was sold to the 'Betton Grange' Society, which intends to use certain parts in a 'new-build' loco. Despite this, the eventual aim of the Society is to restore the engine at its new home on the Llangollen Railway.**

7200 Class 2-8-2T

Typical of many locomotives in the yard, No 7200 has daubed on the side the often vain exhortation 'Do Not Remove Parts'. Purchased for the Quainton Road site, it still awaits restoration thirty-five years after leaving the scrapyard.

4200 Class 2-8-0T

Above **A quintet of ex-GWR motive power is seen in this line-up, those identifiable being Nos 5164, 2857, a 28XX Class 2-8-0 (remarkably, dating from 1918), and 5199, all captured on 14 May 1966.** *GW*

Right **Concluding our GWR section, at the top end of the yard, minus chimney, dome, cylinders, connecting rods and valve gear and no doubt much else, rests this unidentified Prairie tank, still sporting its BR 'cycling lion' emblem on the side tanks. As Jacques in** *As You Like It* **might have said, 'Sans teeth, sans eyes, sans taste … sans everything.'**

Prairie tank

Above **Churchward 4575 Class 2-6-2T No 5541, seen against a background of withdrawn brake vans, is in quite presentable condition after purchase by the Prairie Fund and shortly before removal to the Forest of Dean in October 1972. Restoration was completed in 1975 and it continues to give sterling service there today.**

SOUTHERN REGION

Mogul

Left **SR U Class No 31638 has lost its chimney and was one of four of the class housed at Barry. Purchased by the Bluebell Railway in 1980, it is now matched with a former Schools Class tender base, previously converted for snowplough use, with a new tender tank having been constructed. It steamed for the first time in preservation in 2006.**

Above **Classmate No 31618 had the distinction of being the second locomotive to leave Barry for preservation as early as January 1969, going initially to New Hythe and thence to the Kent & East Sussex Railway, then subsequently to its current home on the Bluebell Railway. The relatively complete nature of the coupling rods and valve gear is explained by the fact that she actually arrived in steam, hauling classmates Nos 31625, 31638 and 31806 from Fratton shed in June 1964. Her boiler ticket expired in 1994 and she is currently in the queue for overhaul.**

Above **The only N Class Mogul to spend time in the scrapyard at Woodham's was No 31874, which had been withdrawn in March 1964 from Exmouth Junction shed, arriving at Barry in June of that year.**

Right **No 31874 is seen shortly after arrival at Alresford in early 1974, courtesy of Aznar Line, which sponsored the move and whose logo is emblazoned on the tender. Aznar Line operated cargo and passenger services from Spain to South America, the United States and the Caribbean. Later it was allocated a large share of the fruit and vegetable market between the Canary Islands and Britain, sailing to both London and Liverpool. In 1974 the first of two large cruise-ferries arrived, one entering service between Southampton and Santander while a sister ship was delivered a year later for summer service between Liverpool and the Canary Islands (Amsterdam–Southampton–Santander in the winter). The locomotive was named *Aznar Line* for a time following restoration. It also carried the name *Brian Fisk* for a while, Fisk Publishing having launched *Mayfair* magazine in 1965. Bachmann also produced a limited-edition OO-scale model of this locomotive with the latter name.**

Above **A recent rain shower adds an almost respectable lustre to the tender of N Class No 31874, which spent almost ten years in the yard before rescue came.**

S15

The massive eight-wheel tender of these S15s shows up to advantage in this view, although it is very apparent how the ravages of time, salt and weather are beginning to take their toll. No 30841 was one of five examples of the Maunsell version of this class in the yard, there also being two examples of the earlier Urie version. All seven examples were subsequently rescued, although two have yet to steam in preservation. Unfortunately the original frames of No 30841 have been found to be out of line and many of the locomotive's components, including the boiler, have been used on No 30825. This problem with the frames does illustrate that sometimes BR did have genuine cause to withdraw a locomotive and it was not always a case of 'making up the numbers' - some were indeed in poor condition and in need of major repair, which was considered uneconomic. Whether it will ever be reconstructed is open to serious doubt and it may now be considered as being essentially scrapped.

Left and Below **These two views show a pair of S15s, 30828 (*Below*), and 30825 (*Left*). Grey primer has been applied to the cylinders of No. 30828 while all pervading rust seems to be the theme of the less fortunate No 30825.**

Above **No 30499 had 1.25 million miles to its credit when sold to Woodham's in early 1964 for the nowadays paltry sum of £1,040 (£20,000 at 2015 prices). It lost its original 5,000-gallon bogie tender at the end of 1963 and had its replacement 4,000-gallon tender purchased to go with U Class No 31625. Originally intended as a source of spare parts, No 30499 is now under restoration on the Mid Hants Railway in its own right.**

Right **This May 1966 view of S15 No 30825 and U Nos 31625 and 31638 shows the relatively good condition, compared to later years, in which these locomotives were to be found in the mid-1960s. Woodham's was to scrap two S15s, Nos 30512 and 30844, before preservationists could raise funds to purchase them.** *GW*

Bulleid Light Pacific

Coupling rods were a prized item when salvaging parts from the Barry fleet, and in this 1970s view No 34070 *Manston* has managed to retain those on at least one side of the locomotive, but in common with most Bulleid Pacifics it was to lose its tender in the ensuing years. (Several Bulleid tenders were sold to steelworks in South Wales to be used as ingot carriers.) It was to be 1983 before this Battle of Britain engine left for preservation, a return to steam occurring in 2008.

It is hard to believe that the splendour that is currently the operational *Tangmere* was once in such a state. No 34067 carries the usual daubed pleas 'Please Don't Remove Parts' and 'Reserved' in the often vain hope that the scavengers would leave the hulks alone. Dai Woodham estimated that hundreds of thousands of pounds worth of parts were stolen from his stock over the years, and from the condition of some of the carcases one could well believe it. A further view of this locomotive is seen later awaiting restoration at Ropley on the Mid Hants Railway.

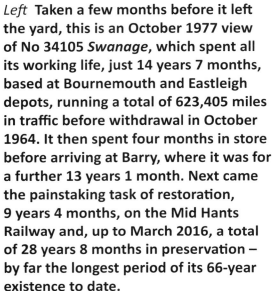

Left Taken a few months before it left the yard, this is an October 1977 view of No 34105 *Swanage*, which spent all its working life, just 14 years 7 months, based at Bournemouth and Eastleigh depots, running a total of 623,405 miles in traffic before withdrawal in October 1964. It then spent four months in store before arriving at Barry, where it was for a further 13 years 1 month. Next came the painstaking task of restoration, 9 years 4 months, on the Mid Hants Railway and, up to March 2016, a total of 28 years 8 months in preservation – by far the longest period of its 66-year existence to date.

Below Left One of the trio of Battle of Britain 'Squadrons' to grace Woodham's yard was No 34072 *257 Squadron*, the rusty marks on the casing sides indicating where the nameplate and squadron crest had once been located. The locomotive now forms part of the Southern Locomotives Ltd fleet, which comprises, among other locomotives, four more Bulleid Pacifics. The squadron after which the locomotive was named flew Hurricanes from RAF Northolt during the Battle of Britain and was finally disbanded at the end of 1963, some ten months before its namesake was withdrawn from BR metals.

Right **It is painfully apparent that in order to remove the crest from West Country Pacific No 34007** *Wadebridge* **the casing has been crudely cut through. Leaving the yard in May 1981, it was to be a long wait until 2006 before restoration was complete.**

Below Right **No 34073** *249 Squadron* **is seen in the mid-1980s in a condition indicative of the state of much of the stock by this date, having been exposed to the elements for more than twenty-five years. Purchased for the abortive Brighton Works Project, it subsequently moved to the Mid Hants Railway. From there it went to Bury, and later to Carnforth, having donated part of its valve gear to sister locomotive** *Tangmere*, **which had suffered a catastrophic failure while hauling a main-line excursion. Its future is currently uncertain.**

The carcases of rebuilt and original Pacifics face each other in 1986 at Luens Bank, Barry, the site where Woodham's began cutting in 1959. On the left is Merchant Navy No 35009 *Shaw Savill* and on the right Battle of Britain No 34073 *249 Squadron* again, but by now shorn of its streamlined casing. Having offered No 35009 for sale a few years ago and attracting no buyers, Ian Riley Engineering has decided to restore it in-house. If you were to visit this location today you would be in the Premier Inn hotel!

A foreground of wagon wheels represents the primary focus of Woodham's cutting activities, the scrapyard's attention switching fortunately to the scrapping of thousands of BR wagons, thereby granting the locomotives sufficient time in limbo for rescue plans to be mounted for the vast majority. A large number of track panels were also dealt with, leading to a further reprieve in locomotive cutting when the supply of wagons had temporarily dried up. Nos 34070 *Manston* and 34046 *Braunton* are cab-to-cab in the background.

No 34101 *Hartland* carries the legend 'Sold 15.7.77', but it was to be another year before it departed from the yard for Shaws Metals Ltd at Derby, having been purchased for use on the Peak Railway. It subsequently moved to the Great Central Railway, where restoration was completed in 1993. It has since moved to the North York Moors Railway, where it is currently under overhaul.

A vivid illustration of the all-consuming rust that attacked the stock at Barry is No 34028 *Eddystone*, which spent twenty-two years at the mercy of the elements here. Of note is the backing plate on the running board where the name was formerly mounted. Typical of the scandalously short life of these rebuilds, this locomotive managed only 5 years and 9 months in service in this modified form.

'When will "Sidmouth" steam again ?' ran the headline in the *Sidmouth Herald* on 11 April 2011. Although rescued from the yard in 1982, thirty-four years on No 34010 is still very much a kit of parts with the frames in Swanage, the boiler at Bridgnorth and many components in various stages of restoration at the Swanage Railway's Herston Works. The amount of money required to restore Barry 'wrecks' is phenomenal, with No 34010 needing £150,000 worth of work on the boiler alone.

After a thirty-one-year stay, the appearance of No 34058 *Sir Frederick Pile* has been superficially improved by the application of primer and paint. Removed in 1986 to the Avon Valley Railway, it was transferred to the Mid Hants Railway in July 2011 for the completion of its restoration.

Left In comparison with the black & white view on page 76, taken in the mid-1960s, No 34027 *Taw Valley* looks rather down-at-heel some fifteen years later. In spite of the Mid Hants appellation inscribed on the running plate, it was in fact purchased privately for the North York Moors Railway initially, being the 112th locomotive to escape the yard. Following moves to Hull and finally to the Severn Valley Railway, it was steamed in preservation for the first time in 1989 and has since run on the main line on many occasions. Interestingly, it has also operated in the guise of scrapped classmate No 34045 *Ottery St Mary*, which, together with No 34094 *Mortehoe*, was one of only two Bulleid Pacifics scrapped by Woodham's. Following the successful rebuilding of No 34005 *Barnstaple* in June 1957, Nos 34027 and 34003 *Plymouth* were the next pair to be converted three months later.

Left Buddleia, so characteristic of railway sidings and barren ground, frames No 34059 *Sir Archibald Sinclair*. Together with many examples, this locomotive lost its tender during its stay. The locomotive was restored to steam in 2009 on the Bluebell Railway.

Merchant Navy

Right **A smoke deflector rests against the bogie truck of No 35006 *Peninsular & Oriental SN Co*, one of ten Merchant Navy Class to be found in the yard. It was steamed for the first time in preservation in August 2015 on the Gloucestershire & Warwickshire Railway.**

Below Right **No 35027 *Port Line* is one of only three Merchant Navy Pacifics to have so far steamed in preservation, the others being Nos 35028 Clan Line, bought direct from BR in 1967, and 35005 *Canadian Pacific*.**

Above Still exuding a sense of power in spite of its condition, No 35011 *General Steam Navigation* awaits rescue, which would come in March 1989 when it achieved the distinction of being the final Merchant Navy to leave the yard bound for the Brighton Works Project. Note that the position of the former badge and nameplate is still apparent on the boiler casing. It is currently on a site in Kent awaiting long-term restoration.

Right With a foreground of rusting corrugated iron and assorted debris, a Merchant Navy Pacific remains unidentifiable thanks to the missing cabside sheets, which reveal only the first two numbers '35'; however, it is believed to be No 35025 *Brocklebank Line*, which had been due to be next in line for cutting after No 92085 had met its end in 1980. Fortunately fate intervened and locomotive cutting ceased due to a further influx of wagons. Alongside is Standard Class 5 No 73096, now resident on the Mid Hants Railway.

Moved to North Woolwich in January 1985, No 35010 *Blue Star* was subsequently transferred to static display at the Colne Valley Railway which, although under threat of closure, was granted a one year extension on its lease of land at Castle Hedingham in July 2015.

Cheek-to-cheek, the similarity between the cabs of a Merchant Navy in the shape of No 35022 *Holland America Line* and a West Country, No 34101 *Hartland*, can readily be seen. Perhaps the most striking difference is the length of the cab side window, noticeably longer on the light pacific.

IN CLOSE-UP

Left A severed wheel, which was cut through with an oxyacetylene torch following a shunting accident that saw the locomotive derailed in the scrapyard, did not hinder the restoration of King Class No 6023 *King Edward II*. Once considered a hopeless case and daubed with the tag 'We Can't Save This One', the pundits were to be proved wrong and once again a preservation resurrection miracle has been achieved. In addition to the preserved *King George V*, two further examples of the class survived, Nos 6023 and 6024, for, unlike the majority of their classmates, which were quickly scrapped following withdrawal, a lucky chance saw them used as dead weights for a bridge test, thus prolonging their existence and ultimately enabling them to find their way to Woodham's yard. Other locomotives also suffering the indignity of cut wheels while in the yard were Jubilee Class No 45699 and 9F No 92207.

Above Greenery could also attach itself to valve gear, as evidenced in this shot of Standard tank No 80104.

As this view of No 73082 *Camelot* attests, grease aplenty was applied to moving parts on reserved locomotives in an effort to inhibit corrosion and to assist in moving them. Movements by rail from Barry to preservation sites came to an end in 1976, after which time road hauliers assumed the task.

The unmistakeable Bulleid-Firth-Brown 'Boxpok' wheels of an SR Pacific.

Above **Weathering of the tender side of an S15 has revealed previous incarnations of this locomotive, with the 'SO' of 'SOUTHERN' showing through, together with older and newer versions of the BR emblem.**

Left **Salvaged rods are partially hidden from prying eyes on the top of the tender of this S15.** *R Thornton*

Right **Numbers ... numbers...**

A close-up of the cylinders and valve gear of Stanier 8F No 48173. The outline left by the builder's plate is apparent on the far left.

Chimneypiece – for the record, they belonged to Nos 5538, 5572, 35009 *Shaw Savill* and 7822. *GW*

MONOCHROME INTERLUDE

Left **S15 No 30825 keeps company with Maunsell Moguls Nos 31625 and 31638. This S15 was the oldest of the Maunsell variants to reach Barry, having been constructed in April 1927 and lasting in traffic until January 1964.**

Below Left **Behind a row of wagon chassis, this is Jubilee Class No 45690 *Leander*. This locomotive made the journey from Bristol's Barrow Road shed, arriving in the yard in June 1964. Dead engines being towed were banned from the direct Severn Tunnel route to South Wales, so they had to make the detour via Gloucester. Leander was one of a pair of Jubilees to reach Barry, the other being No 45699 *Galatea*.**

Right **Some thirty-eight pannier tanks were destined for Barry; however, thirty-one of them were subsequently scrapped by Woodham's, leaving just seven in the yard latterly, six of which were destined for preservation, the unfortunate No 3612 having effectively ceased to exist as it was cannibalised as a source of spares on the Severn Valley Railway. This is a line-up of several of the survivors.**

Below Right **No 5541 is the only locomotive whose identity is confirmed in this 1960s view taken in the lower yard. Remarkably, the former GWR 4-6-0 beyond it still has its safety valve bonnet at this time.**

Above **Black & white rendition always seemed particularly to suit images of the Barry collection, and this is perhaps epitomised in this view of No 7027** *Thornbury Castle* **seen in 1968 but showing few signs of serious decay in spite of some four years' residency in the yard.**

Above Right **The valve gear of this 9F is reasonably complete in this mid-1960s view. Like many of the class, No 92207 had an extremely short working life of just 4½ years. Named** *Morning Star* **in 1986, it is currently based at Shillingstone on the former S&D route, a line upon which the 9Fs did sterling work in the early 1960s, awaiting completion of restoration. A brace of original Bulleids can also be seen in this line-up.**

Below Right **Standard tank No 80136 and Merchant Navy Pacific No 35011** *General Steam Navigation* **were both June 1966 arrivals.**

Above **The connecting rods absent in this view of No 34027 *Taw Valley* would have been removed and probably stashed on the tender, or left protruding from the firebox for the journey to the scrapyard. Such journeys were subject to a 25mph speed restriction and stops would be made where convenient, every 25 miles or so, to check for hot axle boxes.**

Left **N Class No 31874 still exhibits the wooden insert placed in the slide bar to inhibit movement of the valve gear linkages for transport to the scrapyard.**

The peeling paintwork of No 34028 *Eddystone*, seen on 29 October 1979, is captured vividly through the black & white medium. With a price of £6,000, this Bulleid Pacific was purchased in 1986 by Southern Locomotives Ltd, which also now owns Nos 34010, 34053, 34070, 34072, 80104 and an 'Austerity' saddle tank. No 34028 left the scrapyard with, among other defects, cracked frames, a badly wasted firebox, shot bearings, a pitted boiler barrel, bent axles, asbestos contamination and, naturally by this date, no tender. Despite all these problems, it was restored and entered service on the Swanage Railway in 2004.

MIDLAND REGION

4F

Fowler 4F classmates Nos 44422 (nearest the camera) and 44123 retain their connecting rods in this view taken in May 1966, some ten months after their arrival. A third member of the class, No 43924, was also a one-time resident. *GW*

A further view of No 44422, allocated to the Somerset & Dorset line between 1950 and 1960. Leaving the yard in the spring of 1977 this 4F moved to the North Staffordshire Railway at Cheddleton. It is unique in being the only left hand drive example remaining. It recently reprised its S&D role by performing in the West Somerset Railway gala held in March 2016.

'Jinty'

Left **'Jinty' No 47324 was one of seven of the class to visit the yard, this example being the fifth to be rescued, finally finding a home on the East Lancashire Railway after stays at both the Mid Hants and Avon Valley.**

Above **Another example of the Fowler 3Fs was No 47298, seen here in the early 1970s prior to removal from the yard in July 1974.**

Ivatt tank

'Sold 21/11/72' says the inscription on the side tanks of Ivatt tank No 41312. It was to be August 1974 before it left for preservation, initially at Caerphilly but latterly moving to the Mid Hants Railway, where it returned to steam in 2000. What is believed to be No 35025 is alongside.

Stanier 8F

Rust-streaked Stanier 8F No 48518 was one of six of this class of 2-8-0s to end up at Barry, their construction dating from the Second World War years. A couple of the sextet lasted in service in the North West until January 1968, the final year of BR steam.

The star on the cabside underneath the number of 8F No 48151 indicates that it had specially balanced wheelsets/motion, enabling it to work fast vacuum-braked goods services. No 48151 is at present the only 8F certified for main-line use, albeit restricted to 50mph, and in 2014 it worked its first train over Shap summit since the end of steam in 1968.

Jubilee

Here is a colour view of No 45690 *Leander*, seen on page 72 in monochrome, taken on 14 May 1966.
GW

Ivatt Class 2

The Ivatt 2MT 2-6-0s were represented by four examples at Barry, the locomotive illustrated being No 46512, which arrived in June 1967, departing in May 1973. It still sports some glass in the cab windows, and much of the valve gear is seemingly complete. It is currently to be found on the Strathspey Railway, now carrying the name *E. V. Cooper Engineer*. In addition to those that were rescued from Barry, there are a further three examples preserved.

With Standard tank No 80151 behind, another Ivatt 2-6-0 in the shape of No 46428 is parked against the buffer stops in the lower yard.

'Crab'

Two Hughes Class 5 'Crab' 2-6-0s graced the yard, and seen here in company with a couple of pannier tanks is No 42765. Leaving after eleven years at Barry, it moved initially to the Keighley & Worth Valley Railway, but it can now be found on the East Lancashire Railway, where it returned to traffic after overhaul in 2014 resplendent in crimson lake livery as No 13065.

The massive cylinders of this class can be seen to advantage in this view of the other 'Crab' resident at Barry, No 42859, which has had a rather chequered career in preservation. It has been stored at RAF Binbrook in a dismantled state since 1995 while the owner undertook its restoration. However, in November 2012, after the driving wheels and tender frame were removed without the owner's permission, an injunction was obtained to prevent any further removal of parts. The driving wheels were later discovered by the police during a raid on a nearby industrial unit in an unrelated operation, and the owner of the premises was served with a notice preventing the wheels' removal. In June 2013 it was announced that the matter had been classified as a civil dispute by Lincolnshire Police and will have to be pursued through the courts. The boiler and frames were removed from storage in Binbrook under police supervision and moved to a secret location. Legal proceedings for the return of the wheels and tender frame are currently under way. Meanwhile the boiler was subsequently cut up in a Nottingham scrapyard, having been sold by the owner to pay for the costs of moving it from Binbrook. The owner stated that the boiler was beyond economic repair and that he has retained sufficient parts to allow a replacement to be built. The wheels remain at RAF Binbrook under a court order. The locomotive is possibly a lost cause, at least in the short term.

S&D 7F

The former S&D 7F 2-8-0, No 53808, was withdrawn from Bath Green Park shed in 1964, one of the pair that famously escaped the scrapman and made it to Barry and ultimate preservation, first at the abortive Radstock site, but now safely on the West Somerset Railway.

Thirty years on from this view, No 53809 was to revisit the scene of its former triumphs for the 40th anniversary of the closure of the Somerset & Dorset line in March 2006 at Green Park station in Bath.

EASTERN REGION

B1

The sole example of Eastern Region steam to arrive at Barry was Thompson B1 No 61264, seen here in red primer with a chimney covering prior to exit from the yard in July 1976. Although withdrawn in December 1965 the loco was transferred to Departmental service as a mobile boiler for heating carriages until July 1967, and it was in the guise of Departmental No 29 that it arrived in South Wales in September 1968.

BR STANDARD CLASSES

Duke Of Gloucester

Dubbed 'Mission Impossible', the restoration of unique Standard Class 8 No 71000 *Duke of Gloucester* scaled new heights in locomotive preservation. Although BR had listed the locomotive for official preservation as part of the National Collection, for reasons that are now unclear the decision was rescinded and merely one sectioned cylinder together with its associated rotary valve gear was retained. The right-hand cylinder was removed at Crewe Works and used as a 'guinea pig' for the final sectioning of the left-hand cylinder, which was later exhibited at the Science Museum in London, although now located at the Heritage Centre, Crewe. Initially towed to Cashmore's yard at Newport, the gutted remains of the locomotive were spotted by an eagle-eyed former BR fireman, who noticed that the destination label on 'The Duke' read 'Woodham's, Barry'. The rest, as they say, is history. This view was taken shortly after arrival at its correct destination in October 1967 in its 'filleted' state.

Class 4 4-6-0

Standard Class 4MT 4-6-0 No 75069 was one of four of the class to spend time at Barry. Rescue came in March 1973 when it moved to the Severn Valley Railway, as the 'Reserved SVR' markings on the tender, cylinders and running plate would indicate. This was the ninth locomotive to move from Barry to this preservation site up to that time.

Class 2 2-6-0

Not BR Black nor BR Green but 'Vivid Rust' is now the livery worn by a Standard Class 2MT 2-6-0, of which four examples were to be found in the yard.

Class 4 2-6-4T

A line of box vans are also awaiting scrap next to Standard tank No 80104. No fewer than fourteen classmates accompanied it to Woodham's yard, one of which, No 80067, was scrapped. Today No 80104 can be found on the Swanage Railway.

Brighton Works-built classmate No 80150 moved to the Mid Hants Railway in 2011 as part of a deal with Glamorgan Council in return for the MHR's former Bricklayers Arms turntable, which the Council intends to install at Barry as part of its plan to turn it into a main-line steam destination.

A trio of Standard tanks in the shape of Nos 80100, 80097 and 80150 are seen in this view dating from May 1966. *GW*

Class 9F 2-10-0

Looking pretty complete in this 1966 view, No 92219 even has one of its cabside window glasses intact, having arrived in the yard only seven months previously. Purchased originally by the Peak Railway, it subsequently moved to the Midland Railway Centre, where its future as anything other than a set of spares was in doubt until a recent move saw it arrive at the Stainmore Railway's Kirkby Stephen site. Originally outshopped in January 1960 and concurrent with No 92220 *Evening Star*, it managed only 5 years and 7 months in BR service. *GW*

9F No. 92085 joined the ranks of the unlucky pair of Riddles 2-10-0s which were scrapped by Woodham's, the other being No. 92232. Scrapping came late, in 1980 in fact, for this locomotive seen here in the late 1970s alongside Bulleid Pacific No. 34058 which met a happier fate in preservation on the Bluebell Railway.

A further view of the doomed 9F. Only four of the BR Standard designs were scrapped at the yard.

DIESELS

No D6122 – or was it D6121, as suggested by erosion over the years revealing that number on the cab? –was one of the problematical North British Type 2 Class 21s. After a relatively short working life it was moved from Scotland's Inverurie Works in November 1967 and thence to Hither Green on the SR for use in re-railing exercises. It was officially withdrawn from there on 30 December 1967 and, following six months of storage, was sold to Woodham's in June 1968, arriving at Barry on 1 November 1968. It remained there until scrapped in the summer of 1980.

Above **A closer view of the gutted shell of No D601, which spent less than ten years operating on the WR of BR before its premature end. It outlasted its other Warship classmate at Barry by some ten years, not being scrapped by Woodham's until the summer of 1980.**

Below **'The usurper trumped!' might be the caption for this view. A pair of NBL Warship diesels, No D600 *Active* in Rail Blue livery and No D601 *Ark Royal* still in BR green, ended their days at Barry, being scrapped together with two other main-line diesels, Nos D8206 and D6122. The Class 15, D8206, was seldom photographed and, having entered the yard in September 1968, was quickly scrapped in February 1970.**

FREIGHT STOCK

Less glamorous than the locomotive side, Woodham's bread-and-butter business came from scrapping innumerable redundant freight vehicles. In the 1980s, for example, the yard was filled with brake vans now no longer required in an era of fully-fitted freight trains, this view dating from 5 May 1980. This 20-ton example, built at Darlington in 1951, is typical of the thousands that once plied the BR network, and carries the unambiguous markings 'COND' for condemned and 'W' for withdrawn.

Covered Carriage Truck No M94910, dating from 1961, was one of many similar vehicles to be dealt with by Woodham's. This example, photographed on 1 August 1981, was one of more than 800 built by BR at Earlestown Works for general use as parcels vans. They were relatively short-lived, condemnation coming in the early 1980s, although some eked out a further existence in engineering use.

The yellow circle on the side of this van indicates its former use for the carriage of bananas, a traffic that by the end of the 1960s was in decline due to changing distribution requirements and the increased efficiency of road transport following changes in road regulation. These vans were then increasingly used for general goods traffic and marshalled into ordinary goods trains. They were painted bauxite and carried a yellow disc about 18 inches in diameter to the left of the body side with the tare weight of the vehicle written on it in black. The final move from rail to road haulage was made in 1979, rendering the last seventeen operational banana vans redundant. BR built two distinctive designs of banana van in 8- and 12-ton capacities, initially following LMS practices. This example, No 070873, seen at Barry on 15 May 1982, is of the 8-ton vertical wooden plank variety. Some had further careers as barrier wagons, but this was short-lived when air braking became the norm. Judging by the inscriptions on the side of this example, it seems to have been in Civil Engineers' departmental use latterly.

Above **From the chalked holding point 'Cripple Sdngs', a 12-ton mineral wagon, apparently built at Wolverton Works in 1957 and typical of the many thousands that passed through Woodham's yard, has reached its final destination of Barry Docks, as shown on the label marked 'For Breaking Up'. In all, BR was to get rid of 650,000 wagons as part of the 1955 Modernisation Programme.**

Above **This six-wheeled tank wagon was once used for milk, but now No ADE 70355 awaits its fate at Woodham's in January 1982, carrying the prohibition on its tank 'Not to be used for milk'. By 1981 BR had lost this once lucrative traffic and many dedicated wagons were withdrawn, although some saw further internal use carrying a variety of other liquids such as lubricating oil.**

A 22 ½ ton Presflo wagon, B888597, seen at Barry in 1982. In the early 1950's 'air fluidisation' systems were developed for handling fine grained powders such as cement causing them to behave much like a liquid which could then be pumped or drained from a wagon easily. Introduced in 1954 BR built their 'Presflo' wagons for such traffic and from the mid 1960's some of these Presflo wagons were used to carry fly ash from power stations to land fill sites in block trains. They had all be withdrawn from traffic by 1987.

A graphic illustration of the cutting process on a wagon reveals the underframe of a box van.

DOWN THE ROAD AT NEWPORT

Left **The scrapyards of J. Cashmore and J. Buttigieg at nearby Newport represented the other end of the scrapping spectrum from Woodham's in that they generally disposed of locomotives much more quickly on receipt, allowing precious little time for any preservation appeals to be successful. The cab of Standard Class No 92157 is pretty much all that is recognisable here among the fireboxes, smokeboxes and general clutter. No 92157 was one of eleven members of the class dealt with by Buttigieg, which in total cut in excess of 100 locomotives.**

Below Left **Having been based at Derbyshire's Williamthorpe Colliery for some time, 'Jinty' No 47289 was withdrawn from service towards the end of 1967 and promptly scrapped by Buttigieg in February 1968, shortly after this view was taken.**

Stanier 8F No 48395 was next in line for the cutting torch in February 1968. Built at Horwich Works in May 1945, among its allocations were Normanton, Kirkby-in-Ashfield and Edge Hill, from where it was withdrawn in September 1967.

Left **West Country Pacific No 34098 *Templecombe* was withdrawn one month before the end of steam on the SR, being stored on Salisbury dump for some three months before travelling to meet its end in Buttigieg's scrapyard shortly afterwards.**

Below Left **Waiting to enter Cashmore's yard is Standard tank No 82031. Ironically this Swindon-built 3MT tank's first allocation was Barry – if only it had made it back there at the end, perhaps it too would have been saved. As it is, none of forty four-strong class made it into preservation, but it is hoped that the new No 82045, currently under construction at Bridgnorth, will rectify this situation. Cashmore's at Newport accounted for the dispatch of well over 800 locomotives.**

PRESERVATION POSTSCRIPT

Left **This was the method of transport for Barry escapees after the 1976 diktat that no further movements by rail would be allowed. Stanier 8F No 48624 is seen en route to Matlock on the Peak Railway in July 1981 aboard one of the vehicles of Mike Lawrence, a name that has become synonymous with locomotive removals. No 48624 returned to traffic in May 2009 and has since moved to the Great Central Railway, where it is to be seen in crimson livery.**

Below Left **Seen at Ropley on the Mid Hants Railway is No 34067 *Tangmere*, prolifically advertising the name of the local firm that assisted in funding its transport from South Wales.**

Left **Partially under wraps at Ropley is No 34105 *Swanage*, which arrived here in March 1978. Having returned to operational condition in 1987 the locomotive has worked regularly on the Mid Hants Railway but is currently under overhaul at Ropley.**

Below Left **Liberally daubed with slogans is U Class No 31625 seen in 'scrapyard condition' at Ropley, indicative of the challenge ahead to restore such Barry escapees to operational status.**

A final view of the scrap lines at Barry, not so much a graveyard more a birthplace for much of today's preserved steam. Cabsides are seen through the rows of moribund locomotives, including Standard Class 9F No 92212, an unidentified rebuilt Bulleid Pacific and Standard Class 4 No 76077.

Barry Factfile

- Between 1959 and 1968 Woodham Brothers purchased 289 ex-BR steam locomotives together with six ex-MOD steam locomotives and four BR diesels.

- The first locomotives to arrive were five from Swindon Nos 3170, 5312, 5360, 5392 and 5397 in March/April 1959.

- The first locomotive to be rescued was No 43924, which left the yard in September 1968 for the Keighley & Worth Valley Railway.

- The last locomotive to leave was No 4553 in January 1990 for the Dean Forest Railway.

- Only 75 steam locomotives were scrapped together with a half dozen ex-MOD Austerity and four BR diesels. 213 locomotives have been rescued of which 143 have returned to traffic as at mid-2015.

- Oldest locomotive was No 2807, a Churchward 2800 Class dating from 1905; the newest, BR Standard 9F No 92219 built 1960.

- The most numerous class of locomotives to enter the yard were the Bulleid Light Pacifics of which twenty were bought but only two – Nos 34045 *Ottery St. Mary* and 34094 *Mortehoe* – were scrapped.

- The four BR diesels that were at one time located in the yard were Nos D600 *Active*, D601 *Ark Royal*, D6122 and D8206.

- Having been sold to Woodham's by BR, Merchant Navy No 35029 *Ellerman Lines* was repurchased for sectioned display at the National Railway Museum. It was sectioned in 1974 at Sewstern on the ex-British Steel iron ore quarry lines at the end of the High Dyke branch, close to the ECML south of Grantham, with finishing being undertaken at Market Overton.

- Total number of locomotives in the yard in 1968, excluding those to be scrapped subsequently in 1972, 1973 and 1980:

GWR	98
SR	41
LMS	35
LNER	1
BR Standard	38
TOTAL	**213**

- Dai Woodham (5 September 1919–12 September 1994) was awarded the MBE in 1987 in recognition of a number of business initiatives which helped to create many job opportunities in the Barry Docks area.

Renaissance at Ropley: No 34105 *Swanage* restored to active service.

Index

DIESELS
  D600 ACTIVE 103
  D601 ARK ROYAL 103
  D6122...18, 102
EASTERN
  B1
    61264..92
FREIGHT STOCK
  BRAKE VAN 104
  CCT 105
  BANANA VAN 106
  MILK TANK 107
  PRESFLO 108
  12T MINERAL 109
MIDLAND ....
  3F JINTY
    47289...110
    47298...81
    47324...80
  4F
    44123...78
    44422...79
  CRAB
    42765...88
    42859...14, 89
  IVATT CL. 2
    46428...87
    46512...86
  IVATT TANK
    41312...82
  JUBILEE
    45690 LEANDER 72, 85
    45699 GALATEA 24

S&D 7F
  53808..90
  53809..91
STANIER 8F
  48151..84
  48173...69, 70
  48395...111
  48518..83
  48624...113
STANIER BLACK FIVE
  45491..11
SOUTHERN
  BULLEID LIGHT PACIFIC
    34007 WADEBRIDGE 12, 51, 69
    34010 SIDMOUTH 56
    34027 TAW VALLEY 11, 58, 76
    34028 EDDYSTONE 55, 77
    34039 BOSCASTLE 5
    34046 BRAUNTON 18, 53
    34058 SIR FREDERICK PILE.....................57
    34059 SIR ARCHIBALD SINCLAIR..............58
    34067 TANGMERE 49,113
    34070 MANSTON..........................12, 48, 53
    34072 257 SQUADRON...........................50
    34073 249 SQUADRON.......................51, 52
    34098 TEMPLECOMBE...........................112
    34101 HARTLAND...........................54, 63
    34105 SWANAGE 50, 114, 117
  MAUNSELL MOGUL
    31618...41
    31625...47, 114
    31638...40, 47
    31874...42, 43, 76

MERCHANT NAVY
  35006 PENINSULAR & ORIENTAL SN Co. 59
  35009 SHAW SAVILL 52, 71
  35010 BLUE STAR 62
  35011 GENERAL STEAM NAVIGATION 60, 75
  35018 BRITISH INDIA LINE 19
  35022 HOLLAND AMERICA LINE 17, 63
  35025 BROCKLEBANK LINE 61
  35027 PORT LINE 59
S15
  30499...46
  30825...45, 72
  30828...45
  30841...44
  30847...3
STANDARDS
8P
  71000 DUKE OF GLOUCESTER 93
9F
  92085...100, 101
  92157...110
  92207...75
  92212...115
  92219...99
CLASS 2 2-6-0
  78018...95
  78059...15
CLASS 2-6-2T
  82031...112
CLASS 4 2-6-0
  76077...115
CLASS 4 2-6-4T
  80072...17
  80097...98
  80100...98
  80104...65, 96
  80150...14, 97, 98
  80151...87
CLASS 4 4-6-0
  75069...94

CLASS 5 4-6-0
  73082 CAMELOT 66
  73096...60
  73156...10
WESTERN
2800 CLASS
  2857..38
2884 CLASS
  3845..33
4200 CLASS
  5164..38
  5199..38
4575 CLASS
  5538..71
  5541..39, 73
  5572..71
5600 CLASS
  5637..20
7200 CLASS
  7200..37
CASTLE
  5029 NUNNEY CASTLE 29
  5043 EARL OF MOUNT EDGCUMBE 31
  5080 DEFIANT 30
  7027 THORNBURY CASTLE 28, 74
HALL
  5952 COGAN HALL 36
  7927 WILLINGTON HALL 36
KING
  6023 KING EDWARD II 16, 64
MANOR
  7802 BRADLEY MANOR 34
  7822 FOXCOTE MANOR 71
  7828 ODNEY MANOR 35
PANNIER TANK
  3738..32
  4612..16, 32

Also available

Southern Way Special Issue No 9
Scrapping the Southern
Jeffery Grayer

Scrapping the Southern tells the story
of the disposal of the Southern's steam
locomotive stock with particular emphasis
on the 1960s.
With 100 black and white images and 80 in
full colour, the destruction of these giants
of steam is shown in graphic detail.
Included is a fascinating interview with a
member of BR staff who was physically
involved in the cutting process at
Eastleigh Works from 1957 to 1963. These
intriguingly morbid images document not
only the normal life cycle of birth and decay
but bring home the premature waste of
resources in the rush to rid the railway of
what had for so long been its prime mover.

Binding: Paperback
Dimensions: 273mm x 215mm
Pages: 120
Photos/Illustrations: Over 180 photographs
ISBN 978 1909328 044
Price: £16.50

Available online at www.crecy.co.uk
Order hotline 0161 499 0024